WHEN DISASTER STRIKES!

The USS *Greeneville* Submarine Disaster

Eric Fein

rosen central
the rosen publishing group's

Published in 2003 by The Rosen Publishing Group, Inc.
29 East 21st Street, New York, NY 10010

Copyright © 2003 by The Rosen Publishing Group, Inc.

First Edition

All rights reserved. No part of this book may be reproduced in any form without permission in writing from the publisher, except by a reviewer.

Library of Congress Cataloging-in-Publication Data

Fein, Eric.
 The USS *Greeneville* submarine disaster / Eric Fein. -- 1st ed.
   p. cm. -- (When disaster strikes!)
 Includes bibliographical references (p.   ).
 ISBN: 978-1-4358-8932-3
 1. *Greeneville* (Submarine)--Juvenile literature. 2. *Ehime Maru* (Ship)--Juvenile literature. 3. Collisions at sea--Hawaii--Juvenile literature.
 I. Title. II. When disaster strikes! (New York, NY)
 VA65.G78 F45 2002
 363.12'365—dc21

2001008411

Manufactured in the United States of America

On the cover and title page:
The USS *Greeneville* heads out to sea for the first time since it collided with the *Ehime Maru*, killing nine people.

Contents

Introduction 5

1 Prelude to Disaster 8

2 A Failed Mission 15

3 Coping with Tragedy 24

4 Questions, Answers, and Recovery 30

Conclusion 36

Glossary 41
For More Information 42
For Further Reading 44
Bibliography 45
Index 47

Family members mourn the nine people who drowned after the USS *Greeneville* sank the *Ehime Maru*.

Introduction

The story of the deadly collision between the USS *Greeneville* and the Japanese fishing boat *Ehime Maru* is one filled with painful "what ifs," bad timing, and the fatal disregard of small but important details. At the center of these events is the death of nine Japanese fishermen and students on February 9, 2001. Twenty-six survivors are now forever scarred by their ordeal at sea, and thirty-five families will never be the same.

The day dawned with great promise for those on both vessels. For the crew of the USS *Greeneville*, a nuclear-powered submarine based in Pearl Harbor, Hawaii, it was a day to impress sixteen visiting civilians with the might of the navy's submarine fleet.

The USS *Greeneville* Submarine Disaster

For the fishermen and passengers of the *Ehime Maru*, a training vessel, it was to be another beautiful day at sea in the waters south of the Hawaiian island of Oahu. Thirteen students and two instructors from the Uwajima Fisheries High School were on board to learn about the different aspects of commercial ocean fishing. By 1:45 PM, the day's promise would be shattered when the *Greeneville* abruptly surfaced during a training exercise and collided with the *Ehime Maru*, causing the vessel to sink.

The *Ehime Maru* disaster became the first international incident with which the new United States president, George Walker Bush, was confronted. Under the new Bush administration, relations between the United States and Japan had gotten off to a rocky start

Admiral Thomas Fargo *(left)*, commander in chief of the U.S. Pacific Fleet, shakes hands with Yoshikata Sakurada, vice minister of foreign affairs for Japan, after they met to discuss the sinking of the *Ehime Maru*.

John Hall: Civilian Guest on the *Greeneville*

"There was a very loud noise and the entire submarine shuddered... We saw the [*Ehime Maru*] taking on water and the crew bringing things out. We knew it was going to be a devastating effect."

From NBC's *Today* show

even before the sinking of the *Ehime Maru*. The two countries were dealing with ongoing problems arising from a United States military base on the Japanese island of Okinawa. The rowdy and at times violent behavior of some of the U.S. Marines stationed on Okinawa had raised concerns and sparked anger among local politicians and residents.

Into these already troubled waters steamed the *Greeneville* and the *Ehime Maru*. No one really knows how they will handle a crisis until disaster actually strikes. It is only then that men and women—and nations—learn what they are made of. In the eye of the storm that erupted after the collision between the USS *Greeneville* and the *Ehime Maru*, Commander Scott Waddle had to look inward for answers as to how this disaster could happen on his watch—indeed, on his submarine. The United States government also had to ask itself some hard questions about its procedures for operating a submarine with civilians on board.

Meanwhile, the *Ehime Maru* survivors and the families of the victims were left with many agonizing questions that would never receive a satisfying answer.

1

Prelude to Disaster

On February 9, 2001, the USS *Greeneville* was scheduled to take sixteen civilians out to sea for a few hours and impress them with what a nuclear submarine could do. The trip was part of the United States Navy's Distinguished Visitors Program. The program's goals were to educate the public about the need for submarines and to encourage goodwill between the U.S. Navy and the American public, making American taxpayers more willing to continue to fund costly defense projects.

Prelude to Disaster

On the same morning, the *Ehime Maru* would leave Honolulu Harbor on the final leg of an educational voyage that began in Uwajima, in southern Japan. The ship operated as a floating classroom for high school students interested in learning about commercial fishing. It set sail for Hawaii because the waters there are safe and contain plenty of fish. Though neither crew knew it at the time, the two ships were on a collision course with disaster.

What Is a Submarine?

Submarines are ships that can travel either underwater for long distances or along the water's surface, like regular ships. Though we often think of the submarine as a relatively modern invention, underwater ships have been around for several hundred years. The first workable submarine was built around 1620 by a Dutch scientist named Cornelius van Drebbel. His submarine was a rowboat covered with waterproof hides. During the American Revolutionary War (1775–1783), David Bushnell made a one-person submarine called the *Turtle*. It used a hand-cranked

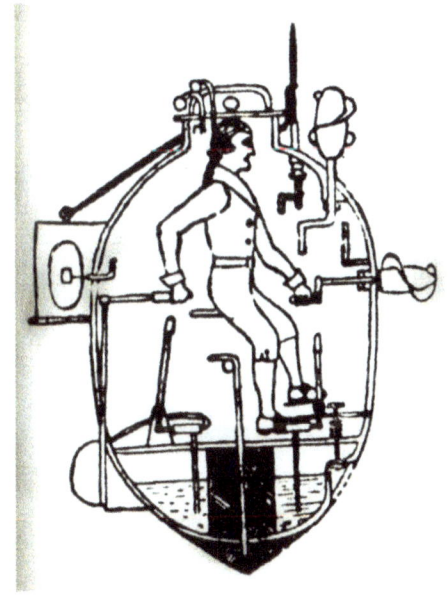

This is the view inside David Bushnell's submarine, the *Turtle*. He used it to try to sink a British warship.

Friday, February 9

7:59 AM

The USS *Greeneville* leaves Pearl Harbor with sixteen civilian guests for a day cruise. Four hours later, the *Ehime Maru* leaves Honolulu Harbor.

propeller to move through the water. The first submarine to sink a vessel in wartime was the Confederate submarine the HL *Hunley*, a nine-person vessel powered by hand cranks. During the Civil War, on February 17, 1860, the *Hunley* sank the Union ship the USS *Housatonic* with a 135-pound torpedo. In the process, it too was damaged and sank. Submarines were greatly improved upon following the Industrial Revolution and used to great effect in World War I and World War II.

Today, there are two types of submarines: attack submarines and ballistic missile submarines. Attack submarines, like the USS *Greeneville*, are used to look for and destroy enemy submarines and ships that move on the surface of the ocean. They carry a crew of about 130 people and are armed with torpedoes and guided missiles (which can be fired underwater but burst through the ocean's surface and hit targets on the land and sea). Attack submarines can be from 290 to 360 feet (88 to 110 meters) long.

Ballistic missile submarines are made to attack land targets (enemy cities and military bases). The missiles carried by this type of submarine can hit targets that are from 1,500 to 4,000 miles (2,400 to 6,400 kilometers) away. Ballistic missile submarines are bigger than attack submarines, ranging in length from about 380 to 560 feet (115 to 170 meters) long. They usually carry a crew of about 150 people.

Prelude to Disaster

How Submarines Work

A submarine can go deep under the water by filling its ballast tanks with water. Ballast is weight that is added to a ship to increase its stability and control. When water fills a submarine's ballast tanks, it makes the submarine heavier. This added weight allows the submarine to submerge. When it is time for a submarine to resurface, the added water in the ballast tanks is pushed out with the aid of compressed air. Now the submarine is lighter and can rise to the surface.

Lieutenant Commander and Executive Officer John Mosier is pictured in the control room of the USS *Columbia*, the USS *Greeneville*'s sister ship.

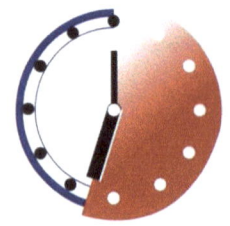

Friday, February 9

12:32 PM

The *Ehime Maru* is first spotted by the *Greeneville*'s sonar, and its position is noted by Petty Officer Patrick Seacrest.

Submarine Chain of Command

Submarines are worlds unto themselves, involving an elaborate system of command and very specialized tasks. A submarine is a very complex and dangerous vessel, and it must be run in an orderly, precise way. If each and every member of the crew is not performing his (women are still not allowed to serve on U.S. Navy submarines) specific task properly, the entire ship is jeopardized.

The person in charge of and responsible for each crew member is the submarine's commanding officer (CO). It is the CO's duty to make sure that the sub and her crew carry out whatever mission they are assigned in a responsible and efficient way.

Hisao Onishi: Captain of the *Ehime Maru*

"All of a sudden, oil and vapor just blew up in the engine room... I hoped others were still in the ocean. We looked for people hard, but I couldn't rescue anyone. We did our best to find other survivors. We just couldn't find the nine missing."

From the *Honolulu Advertiser*

Prelude to Disaster

The second in command on a submarine is the executive officer. The executive officer, or XO as he is usually called, is responsible for coordinating the administrative and training activities of the submarine. Below the commanding officer and the executive officer are department heads and division officers whose responsibility it is to oversee the day-to-day operation of the submarine by supervising the watches—or work shifts—and the work centers.

Each watch section is run by the officer of the deck (OOD), who makes sure that the commanding officer's orders are carried out. The engineering officer of the watch monitors the sub's nuclear reactor and all engineering concerns. The diving officer of the watch, who is usually a chief petty officer, directs the submerging and rising of the ship and also monitors the ship's control party—the people who are responsible for making sure torpedoes and missiles hit their targets.

Commanding Officer Scott Waddle was reprimanded and ordered to resign by the commander of the U.S. Pacific Fleet. Waddle was found guilty of dereliction of performance of duties and of negligent hazarding of a vessel. The decision effectively ended his career.

The USS *Greeneville* Submarine Disaster

The Commanding Officer of the Greeneville

Scott Waddle graduated from the Annapolis Naval Academy in 1981. He never intended to join the submarine service but instead wanted to be a fighter pilot like his father, Dan Waddle, a retired air force colonel.

Unfortunately, his eyesight was not good enough to be a pilot. He could not pass the vision test. It was only when he realized that he would never become a pilot that he turned his attention to submarines.

Waddle worked his way up through the navy ranks until he received his own submarine to command. Waddle was well liked by his crew. According to *Time* magazine, he had the highest reenlistment rate (65 percent) of any attack sub in the Pacific Fleet, meaning that most of his crew wanted to continue to serve under him after their required period of service was over.

In addition to being an effective and caring commander of his crew, Waddle was also a politically savvy person. He understood the power of maintaining a good image both with his superiors and with the public. He worked hard to make himself and his ship a good advertisement for the navy. It was this enthusiasm for charming and pleasing people that would contribute to the fatal mistakes made on February 9, 2001.

2

A Failed Mission

The *Greeneville*'s mission on February 9, 2001, was part military exercise, part pleasure cruise, and part public relations tour. It was a mission of several goals, therefore, many of them contradictory. The very serious and intricate military maneuvers at the heart of the excursion—maneuvers that required very focused attention to detail—would be compromised by the day's other goals: to entertain and impress the ship's civilian guests. The consequences of this failed mission would prove to be fatal.

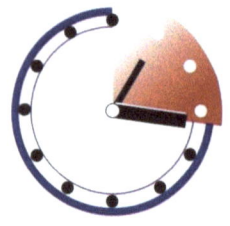

Friday, February 9

1:16 PM

Running forty-three minutes late, the *Greeneville* quickly executes various vertical and horizontal turns to demonstrate the ship's maneuvering abilities.

Running Late

Commander Waddle spent lunchtime entertaining his civilian guests. After lunch, which ran late, Waddle went to his cabin to autograph photos of the *Greeneville* to give to the visitors as mementos. Around 1 PM, the executive officer notified him that they were running forty-five minutes behind schedule for their return to Pearl Harbor. They were supposed to meet with the tug that would bring them back into the harbor at 3 PM. Waddle told his executive officer not to worry; he would take care of things. At that point, the *Greeneville* was about twelve to thirteen miles away from the entrance to Pearl Harbor.

A few minutes later, in the control room, Waddle began the afternoon's activities. He took the *Greeneville* through a series of fast maneuvers to show the civilian observers how a submarine evades torpedoes. The maneuvers consisted of rapid changes of depth and sudden high-speed turns. These maneuvers are commonly called "angles and dangles."

After that, Waddle and his crew prepared for an emergency main ballast blow. As the "angles" demonstration was coming to an end, Commander Waddle told the officer of the deck, Lieutenant j.g. (junior grade) Michael Coen, to take the *Greeneville* to periscope depth in five minutes. Periscope depth is a depth equal to the length of a periscope (depending on the periscope, this can range from

A Failed Mission

about twenty-four to sixty feet). Normally this task would take at least eight minutes to complete. At the same time, the crew was using the *Greeneville*'s sonar equipment to listen for any approaching ships that would have to be avoided.

How Sonar Works

Submarines use sonar to detect and locate nearby objects and other vessels underwater. Submarines use two types of sonar: active and passive. Active sonar uses a sound wave that is sent from the submarine and travels through the water. If the sound wave encounters something, it will bounce off the object and return to its point of origin. These returning echoes let the submarine crew know the object's location. Using active sonar can be risky, since the signal it sends out gives away the submarine's position, allowing enemy ships to determine its location. Passive sonar has to do with listening. The submarine uses special microphones, called hydrophones, to listen for the sounds of another submarine's or ship's propellers or engines. Since no signals are sent out, passive sonar does not reveal the position of the submarine that is using it.

Sailors in a submarine's red-lit sonar room, like this one on the USS *Atlanta*, must focus all of their attention on their duties.

The USS *Greeneville* Submarine Disaster

Communication Breakdown

Petty Officer Patrick Seacrest was responsible for keeping both Waddle and Coen aware of any ships in the area. More than an hour before the accident, Seacrest detected a sonar pattern 15,000 yards away, indicating the presence of a boat. He named the sonar contact Sierra 13. Sierra 13 would turn out to be the *Ehime Maru*. The next time he checked on Sierra 13, it had moved to within 4,000 yards of the *Greeneville*. Despite this, he did not alert either Waddle or Coen to the presence of the approaching ship. They were at the periscopes scanning the horizon, trying to visually confirm that there were no other ships nearby. This procedure is supposed to take three minutes to perform, but Waddle and Coen took only half that time to check

Lieutenant Commander John Mosier of the USS *Columbia* demonstrates the use of a periscope.

A Failed Mission

the area. They did not see the *Ehime Maru*. It is thought that the ship, which was white, got lost among ocean swells (very big waves) and against the backdrop of a milky, hazy sky. Commander Waddle commented that everything looked clear.

At the same time, Seacrest still had Sierra 13 on his sonar. A naval observer, Captain Robert Brandhuber, the chief of staff for the Submarine Force, U.S. Pacific Fleet, was also on the *Greeneville* that day. He watched Commander Waddle in action. Brandhuber felt that Waddle was rushing things and considered offering him a gentle and discreet word of caution. In the end, he decided not to because he was concerned about embarrassing Waddle in front of the civilians and his crew. It would be a decision Brandhuber would come to regret.

What further complicated the situation was that all sixteen civilian visitors were crowded into the control room. This made it difficult for Waddle and his crew to communicate easily with one another; there were just too many people in the room getting in the way and possibly distracting the crew.

Commander Waddle, rushing to make up time lost during the long lunch, did not talk with his contact management team (consisting of an officer of the deck, a sonar supervisor, and the fire technician of the watch, or FTOW) before deciding to execute the emergency blow. Yet this team knew that sonar had detected the *Ehime Maru*. Commander Waddle announced that he had "a good feel about the contact situation," which means that he felt assured that the area was clear of ships. He then ordered an "emergency deep"—an evasive maneuver that is meant to prevent a collision while the submarine is at periscope depth and involves a rapid descent. The *Greeneville* descended 400 feet and started to make a turn but did not finish it.

Friday, February 9

1:37 PM

The *Ehime Maru* draws to within 4,000 yards of the *Greeneville*, but Petty Officer Seacrest does not report this to his superiors.

Emergency Surfacing Drill

In mid-turn, Commander Waddle ordered the emergency blow—a very rapid surfacing drill. The point of this exercise is to simulate an accident scenario in which a damaged submarine would have to surface as quickly as possible in order to evacuate its crew safely. The submarine captain uses the sub's sonar to check and see if there are any vessels or ships nearby. Then the sub goes up to periscope depth and the captain looks through the periscope to visually confirm that there are no other ships in the area.

If the area is clear of all traffic, the submarine dives again. Having reached the appropriate depth, highly pressurized air is then injected into the ballast tanks. This expels the hundreds of tons of water stored in the tanks in mere seconds, shooting the sub up and out of the water.

The sixteen civilians who were aboard the USS *Greeneville* during her collision with the *Ehime Maru* are transported back to Pearl Harbor, Hawaii, after the accident.

A Failed Mission

Waddle invited two of the visiting civilians to take part in this procedure under strict supervision. One took up a position to help start the emergency blow; the other sat in the helmsman's seat to help steer the ship. Once they were stationed, the exercise commenced. Waddle announced that the ship was at 400 feet and heading rapidly for the surface. It was 1:43 PM—a moment no one involved would forget.

Sudden Impact

The *Greeneville* shot up to the surface like a rocket. Its rapid ascent was suddenly and violently interrupted, however, as the submarine smashed into the *Ehime Maru*. When Commander Waddle checked the periscope's video monitor, he was horrified to see the *Ehime Maru*

This navy file photo shows crew members manning the sail of the USS *Greeneville* as it surfaces following an underwater run.

The USS *Greeneville* Submarine Disaster

damaged and sinking. The *Greeneville* struck the fishing vessel at 1:43 PM. Commander Waddle described what happened to *Dateline NBC*'s Stone Philips: "[I] felt that first shudder, it was almost a loud bang ... When I heard the first bang, I didn't know what the noise was. And then that was immediately followed by another noise and a shudder and a sensation that we were kind of getting slowed down. And it was at that time, I knew that something was gravely wrong."

The *Greeneville*'s rudder cut through the *Ehime Maru*'s bottom. As the *Greeneville* continued to move away from the scene, Waddle saw the *Ehime Maru* begin to take on water. As its stern (rear) began to sink, its passengers and crew began to scramble forward on deck. Waddle immediately ordered the submarine to reverse its direction and head back to the accident scene. The *Ehime Maru*'s bow (front) was sticking out of the water vertically, and the ship was sinking rapidly. Within just ten minutes, the ship sank out of sight entirely.

Overboard

At the moment of impact with the submarine, the *Ehime Maru* lost its power. The lights went out, and Captain Hisao Onishi could not give the signal to abandon ship. The *Ehime Maru* started to sink almost immediately after being struck. Most of the *Ehime Maru*'s crew were already jumping overboard to swim to the life rafts. Some thought they had been struck by a whale. In the terror of the moment, most forgot to grab life vests.

The *Honolulu Advertiser* reported that after the crash, Commander Waddle got on the *Greeneville*'s public address system and spoke to his crew. He tried to calm them, urged them to trust in their training,

> ### Tommy Kron: Coast Guard Executive Petty Officer
>
> "The only thing we saw was a submarine, some life rafts, and a little bit of debris. It seemed like [the *Ehime Maru* survivors] were in shock. They were fatigued by the time we got there. Some were seasick. They were pretty quiet. I think a lot of them were too seasick to move. Some had swallowed diesel [fuel]. None of them had their life jackets on. Might not have had enough time."
>
> #### From the *Honolulu Advertiser*

and encouraged them to tell the truth during the inevitable investigation that would await them back on land. According to Tony Schnur, one of the visiting civilians on board, Waddle said, "I don't know what this will bring, but you are one of the finest crews I have ever worked with. You know how we operate on this ship. Our code of conduct here is safety, honesty, and integrity. You know, this incident will be fully investigated. We must tell the truth. Remember what you saw, remember what happened, do not embellish. Tell the truth and maintain your integrity."

Michael Mitchell, another visiting civilian from Irving, Texas, told the *Honolulu Advertiser* that after the impact "there was just dead silence." He said, "We were all in shock . . . Everyone was devastated." Schnur's wife, Susan, claimed that Waddle's face turned absolutely white with shock. Later, Waddle would give an autographed photo of the *Greeneville* to each of his sixteen visitors. Even in the wake of a deadly tragedy, he could not stop himself from trying to put a positive spin on the day and gaining favor for the navy.

3

Coping with Tragedy

A hurried order, a rapid surfacing, a moment's confusion, a sudden impact. This chain of split-second actions would suddenly result in a lifetime of enduring sorrow and loss for the participants in the *Greeneville–Ehime Maru* disaster.

Coping with Tragedy

The Coast Guard to the Rescue

As soon as Commander Waddle realized what had happened, the *Greeneville* contacted the command center. CBS News reported that the message was, "Have experienced collision with surface vessel . . . Vessel appears to be taking on water and sinking at this time . . . Have Coast Guard contacted immediately . . . to render assistance."

Within two minutes of receiving the *Greeneville*'s call for help, the Coast Guard station in Honolulu sent rescue boats and helicopters to the scene. The waters were rough, and the ships had to navigate through four- to six-foot waves as quickly as possible. The Coast Guard's helicopter crew was the first on the scene. From above, they saw the *Greeneville*, three life rafts that were linked together, and three other rafts drifting on their own. The only thing left of the *Ehime Maru* was some debris and a slick of diesel fuel. The Coast Guard rescue boats arrived shortly after the helicopters. They wasted no time in searching for people still left in the water. The people in the life rafts, who were coated in diesel fuel, were put on the Coast Guard boats where their injuries were treated and they were given blankets to keep them warm. Sadly, four students, two instructors, and three crewmen—ranging in age from seventeen to sixty—would not be plucked alive from the rough waters.

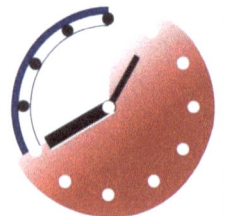

Friday, February 9

1:40 PM

Preparing for an emergency blow, the *Greeneville* begins to descend after Commander Waddle hastily scans surrounding area through the periscope.

"They Didn't Do Enough"

Ehime Maru's survivors claimed that the crew of the *Greeneville* did not do enough to help them as the ship was sinking. Commander Waddle defended his actions, however, by explaining that the seas were very rough and there was a strong wind. This caused the sub to bob upon the choppy waves. Plus, the sub's rounded sides made it impossible for anyone to climb aboard in the rough seas. He explained

U.S. Coast Guard personnel rescue some of the twenty-six survivors from the *Ehime Maru* soon after it was hit by the USS *Greeneville*. The search for survivors covered 10,000 square miles.

Scott Waddle: Commander of the *Greeneville*

> "It is with a heavy heart that I express my most sincere regret. I know that the accident has caused unimaginable grief. No words can adequately express my condolences and concern for those who have lost their loved ones."
>
> **From a letter of apology sent by Waddle to Japan**

to *Dateline NBC*'s Stone Philips, "As we approached one survivor in a life raft, it [the submarine] pushed water in his raft and almost caused him to flip. And with that, I directed the officer of the deck to get [the sub] away from the man. Because we were putting him in greater danger than we were providing him help and assistance."

Jill Waddle, Commander Waddle's wife, spoke to *Dateline NBC*'s Stone Philips about waiting for the *Greeneville*'s return after the accident. There were television cameras and helicopters swarming the area. "You can't hear a submarine when it pulls in, but I could hear all the helicopters," she said. "I knew at that point that this was big and this was going to be hard, and I knew it was the end of his career. I knew that was going to be the last time."

Making Apologies

Commander Waddle wanted to apologize to the families of the victims as soon as possible. He appealed to the public affairs officer of Commander Submarine Force, Pacific Fleet (COMSUBPAC) to allow him to meet the families and apologize in person. The navy and

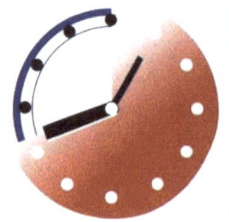

Friday, February 9

1:43 PM

After a rapid ascent to the surface, the *Greeneville* strikes and sinks the *Ehime Maru*.

Waddle's lawyer, Charles Gittins, were both hesitant to grant his request. They thought that the emotions were too raw, the timing wasn't right, and it might appear like an admission of guilt.

Frustrated by the caution of the navy and his lawyer, Waddle took matters into his own hands, writing letters of apology to the family members, the crew members, the captain, the principal of the fishery school, the prefecture of Uwajima, and the prime minister of Japan. Waddle took full responsibility for the disaster. "The buck stops with me," he told *Dateline NBC*'s Stone Philips. "If a shipmate makes a mistake, if a crew member makes a mistake, it's my mistake. I buy it. It's mine."

Scott Waddle *(right)* speaks with talk-show host Larry King during an interview about the accident on CNN's *Larry King Live* show.

The navy called for a court of inquiry to investigate the collision. An inquiry is a military court that inquires into and reports on military matters. Commander Waddle was suspected of dereliction of duty, improper hazarding of a vessel, and negligent homicide. If he was found guilty, he was facing a court

Fumio Yogusuri: *Ehime Maru* Survivor

"I was so frightened. I remember I was moved to the ocean by a big wave. I was in a lifeboat. I don't remember how I got to the boat. I was saved. I was saved. Please find the missing."

From the *Honolulu Advertiser*

martial (a military trial) and years in jail. Commander Waddle was determined, however, to explain to the families and the navy exactly what happened on February 9. He was questioned for six hours, during which every aspect of the actions he took was examined. The main focus of the questioning that day was on the forty-five minutes leading up to the collision. The navy wanted to determine if Waddle had rushed himself and his crew in order to make up lost time, in the process making a series of mistakes that led to the sinking of the *Ehime Maru*.

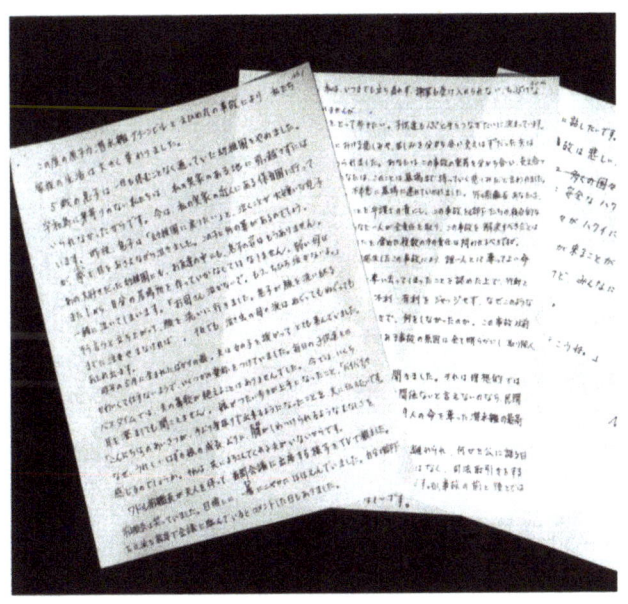

Naoko Nakata, who lost her husband, Jun, in the collision, handed this three-page letter to Scott Waddle after he apologized privately to family members of the *Ehime Maru* victims.

4

Questions, Answers, and Recovery

With the initial silent shock and numb sorrow caused by the sinking of the *Ehime Maru* wearing off, grief, anger, and impassioned calls for justice began to take their place. Attention was turned from the troubled waters south of Oahu to the court of inquiry taking place on shore. The recovery efforts, however, would soon bring the navy back to the scene of the accident.

The Court of Inquiry Findings

Over thirty people testified at the navy's court of inquiry, including Vice Admiral Albert Konetzni, head of the Pacific Fleet's submarine force. Konetzni was not only Commander Waddle's boss but also his close friend. It was painful for him to testify, but he had to. According to the Associated Press, Konetzni testified that Waddle's failure to spot the *Ehime Maru* with the periscope was the direct cause of the crash. He said, "The commanding officer . . . has the absolute obligation to make sure the area is free. That is what caused this collision."

The inquiry found that the collision was caused by several additional factors. First, the *Greeneville* did not perform thorough sonar and visual searches before surfacing. Instead, the crew undertook brief and hurried sonar and periscope searches that did not meet the navy's stringent requirements for such actions.

The second cause of the collision was found to be poor communication among the ship's crew. Vital information concerning nearby ships was not provided to Commander Waddle, partly due to the crowding presence of the visiting civilians. As a result, he had an incomplete picture of what was occurring above the *Greeneville* when he ordered the emergency blow.

The most important cause of the collision—and the miscommunication that gave rise to it—was Commander Waddle's false sense of urgency. He rushed his crew members to do their jobs in less time than required. The sonar operators did not have the time to analyze the data they received and properly track the vessels sailing overhead.

Friday, February 9

3:38 PM

An hour after the first of two Coast Guard boats arrives at the scene, twenty-six survivors of the sunken *Ehime Maru* are rescued, while nine others drown.

Commander Waddle was found guilty of committing two violations of the Uniform Code of Military Justice: dereliction in the performance of his duties and negligent hazarding of a vessel. His punishment was a punitive letter of reprimand (an official criticism of his conduct on the job), and he was relieved of his position as commander of the USS *Greeneville*. While he escaped serving any jail time, the punishment was still severe to this second-generation, lifetime military man: A once promising naval career that spanned twenty years was suddenly cut short.

As part of the investigation into the collision, National Transportation Safety Board (NTSB) inspectors examine the aft (rear) escape trunk on the USS *Greeneville*.

Questions, Answers, and Recovery

In addition to Commander Waddle, other *Greeneville* officers were disciplined. The executive officer, Lieutenant Commander Gerald Pfeifer, was cited for lack of administrative oversight, as was the chief of the boat, Douglas Coffman. The sonar supervisor, Edward McGiboney, was cited for permitting an unqualified sonar operator on watch. The naval observer, Captain Brandhuber, was admonished for not getting actively involved when he saw standard safe operating procedures being disregarded on the *Greeneville*.

The inquiry found that the civilians on board the *Greeneville* did not play a direct role in the accident but that they were a distraction to Commander Waddle and hindered the flow of information in the crucial moments before the deadly accident.

Many Japanese were outraged when Commander Waddle was allowed to leave the navy without serving any jail time. Masami Inoue, a lawyer for one of the families, told the Associated Press, "It's unthinkable that nobody was criminally charged for killing nine people. The Japanese government has been too timid toward the U.S."

Changes to the Visitors Program

The court of inquiry recommended that the Distinguished Visitors Program—the program that allows civilians to board vessels and observe and participate in potentially dangerous military exercises—be run under closer supervision and with approval of the navy's most experienced leaders. Also, in the future, civilians should not be placed in key stations during critical operations, such as emergency blows.

The USS *Greeneville* Submarine Disaster

To Raise the *Ehime Maru*

Using the Scorpio II—a remotely operated vehicle (ROV) that can search underwater areas that divers cannot reach—the navy located the *Ehime Maru* at 11:29 PM on February 16. The *Ehime Maru* was sitting almost upright in about 2,000 feet of water. It had come to rest about 1,000 yards from the site of the accident. The Scorpio II detected the sunken ship with its onboard sonar at 11:25 PM. The confirmation came at 11:29 when the Scorpio II's video cameras were able to read the stern plate that bore the ship's name.

A remotely operated vehicle hovers above the *Ehime Maru* as the sunken fishing vessel is lifted from the ocean floor to a shallow-water recovery site off the coast of Honolulu, Hawaii.

Steven A. Williams: Coast Guard Operations Chief Captain

"We intend to search as long as we believe there is a reasonable hope that we will find survivors and that we will rescue them from this tragic incident. We still think we may find survivors."

From the *Honolulu Advertiser*

The navy hoped to be able to recover the nine missing men right away, but that was not possible. Its remote-controlled surveying gear could not be sent to the site of the wreck for a few days because the weather was bad and the seas too rough for underwater exploration.

Despite the pressure for quick action, the navy could not raise the ship overnight. Raising a ship from 2,000 feet below the surface of the water is no easy task. At that depth, there are about 867 pounds of pressure per square inch placed on the ship, making it very heavy and difficult to hoist. Plus, the navy had to meet with federal and state agencies to determine if raising the *Ehime Maru* would impact the undersea environment around the ship.

In June 2001, the navy announced its plan to search for and recover the nine missing bodies. They wanted to move the *Ehime Maru* to a spot on the seabed shallower than its current location. Moving it would make it safer for navy divers—who could be crushed to death by the enormous pressure of such deep water—to explore its interior.

At the end of August, the navy managed to raise the stern of the *Ehime Maru*. This enabled salvage crews to install equipment to partially raise the boat and move it closer to the shore so divers could try to recover the bodies of the nine men still lost at sea.

Conclusion

Finally, eight months after the Scorpio II first located it, on October 15, 2001, the navy, using at least eight ROVs, successfully moved the *Ehime Maru* across fourteen miles of ocean, up a steep underwater slope, and into its new, shallower resting place. Here, Japanese and American divers could more safely and easily explore it. Moving the damaged 830-ton ship from beneath 2,000 feet of water was an unprecedented naval feat that had never before been done. Yet this was no time for celebration, as divers set to work searching for the remains of the accident's nine victims.

Conclusion

Sensitivity and Recovery

In order to show as much respect as possible for the sensitivities of the victims' families, the navy officers in charge of the recovery effort consulted with George Tanabe, a professor of religion at the University of Hawaii. Most of the *Ehime Maru* victims were Buddhists, and their families had certain spiritual beliefs about burial and the afterlife that the recovery team wished to take into account when planning the operation and its procedures. Their desire to avoid causing further pain to the families extended even to the words they used to describe the mission. For example, they referred to the victims as "the missing" rather than "the bodies," and the mission itself was characterized as a "recovery" rather than a "salvage" operation. After the recovery mission was completed, the navy planned to let the *Ehime Maru* "go to its final resting place" rather than "sink" it.

An unidentified member of the Japanese media *(right)* holds a pair of pants that are among personal belongings recovered by the U.S. Coast Guard from the victims of the *Ehime Maru*.

The USS *Greeneville* Submarine Disaster

The most culturally sensitive aspect of the recovery effort was the handling of the victims' remains. While Americans—and navy sailors in particular—often regard burial at sea as a high honor, many Japanese believe that the body's needs continue on after death, making recovery of remains a critical priority. Professor Tanabe explained in an interview with National Public Radio the importance to the victims' families of recovering the remains of their departed loved ones: "The primary form of ritual care takes the form of feeding. If the dead are not fed, there's also a very common belief they become what are called 'hungry spirits' or 'hungry ghosts.' If you don't have the remains to cremate and keep and to care [for] after death, then there's no closure. The families can never feel that in some way they have fulfilled their responsibility for caring for the dead."

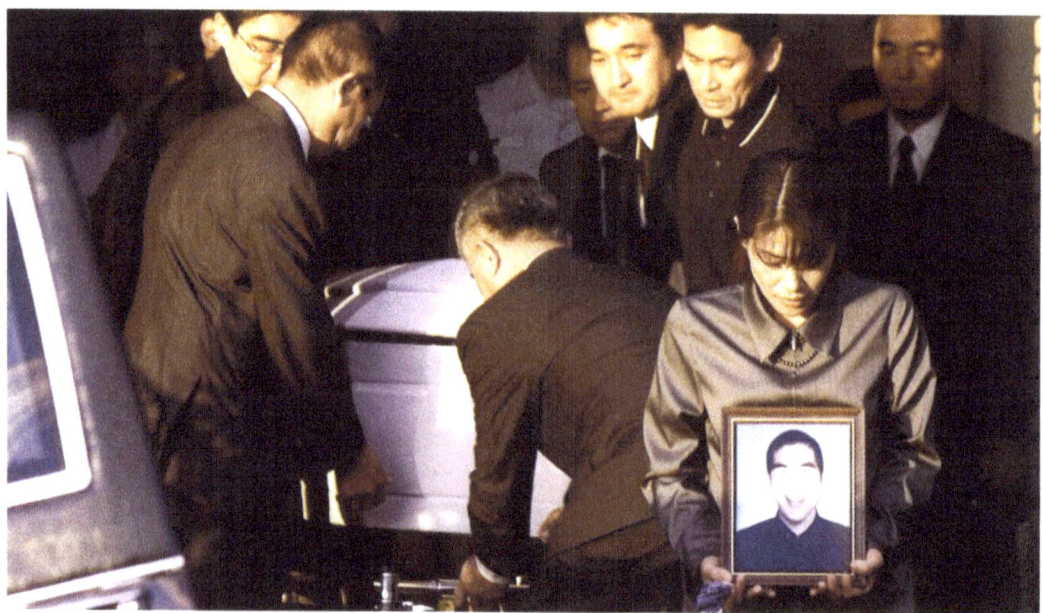

Masumi Terata *(right)* and her husband, Ryosuke, *(directly behind her)* walk before the coffin of their late son, Yusuke Terata, following funeral services on October 31, 2001, at Nuuanu Memorial Cemetery in Honolulu, Hawaii. Yusuke was a student aboard the *Ehime Maru*.

Conclusion

This concern for the care of the body and its spirit extended to the manner in which remains were handled after being found in the water. Navy divers would place the recovered remains in body bags feet first, in accordance with the Buddhist belief that this would help the victim's spirit to remain standing upright. In addition, remains were brought up to the surface only once a day, after sunset, in order to respect the families' privacy. This also allowed the divers and crew to stand at attention and observe a brief memorial ceremony as the victims' remains were being raised.

In the end, the remains of eight of the nine missing men were recovered from inside the *Ehime Maru*. On November 8, 2001, the recovery effort was called off. Only Takeshi Mizuguchi, a seventeen-year-old student, could not be found after a twenty-three-day search that involved 425 dives totaling 333 hours underwater (12 hours a day), at a cost of $60 million. It was decided that he would receive a burial ceremony at sea, after which the *Ehime Maru* would be submerged and come to a final rest 6,000 feet below the ocean's surface. A joint Japanese-American memorial to the *Ehime Maru* will be erected in Hawaii, preserving the memory and the spirits of the nine men forever. This recovery effort is said to have soothed some of the hurt felt by victims' families and restored some measure of trust and friendship between the people of Japan and the United States.

While Takeshi Mizuguchi will forever remain under the waves, Commander Waddle will never return to the sea as a navy sailor. Though initially causing a rift between these men's countries, sorrow has come to replace anger, blame has yielded to forgiveness, and divisions have been smoothed by reconciliation. Masumi Terata, mother of Yusuke Terata, one of the students killed in the accident, bears no

The USS *Greeneville* Submarine Disaster

The Hawaiian voyaging canoe *Hokule* carries flower offerings of lei for the victims of the *Ehime Maru*. It sailed to the scene of the accident with relatives of the missing, who are aboard the modern boat in the background.

ill will toward the crew of the *Greeneville*, whose careless mistakes took her son away from her: "I hold a grudge against the cobalt-blue ocean that took Yusuke's life."

Even Takeshi Mizuguchi's mother expressed no resentment when the recovery mission was called off, and instead chose to focus on her son's enduring spirit. According to the navy's Rear Admiral William Klemm, head of the salvage and recovery mission, as quoted in the *Honolulu Advertiser*, "She felt her son was here in Hawaiian waters and that he was watching this operation and that he would remain in Hawaiian waters to watch out for all of the seamen in this area."

It can only be hoped that a renewed vigilance, thoroughness, and careful attention to detail on the part of the U.S. Navy—and perhaps the watchful and protective gaze of Takeshi Mizuguchi's spirit—will prevent further loss of life in the waters that are now Mizuguchi's resting place.

Glossary

bow   The forward part of a ship.
hull   The body of a submarine.
periscope   A tubular optical instrument containing lenses and mirrors by which an observer obtains an otherwise obstructed field of view.
prefecture   The district governed by a prefect (a chief officer).
rudder   A flat metal structure attached upright to the stern of a submarine.
sonar   A method or device for detecting and locating objects or vessels underwater by means of sound waves sent out and reflected by an object or vessel.
stern   The rear part of a ship.
swells   A long and massive wave or series of waves.

For More Information

All Hands
The Magazine of the U.S. Navy
Superintendent of Documents
U.S. Government Printing Office
Washington, DC 20402
e-mail: allhands@mediacen.navy.mil
Web site: http://www.chinfo.navy.mil/navpalib/allhands/ah-top.html

Ehime Maru Recovery Operation
Public Affairs Officer
(808) 471-3769

For More Information

Naval Historical Center and Museum
Department of the Navy
805 Kidder Breese Street SE
Washington Navy Yard
Washington, DC 20374-5060
Web site: http://www.history.navy.mil/index.html

U.S. Pacific Fleet
Public Affairs Officer
Commander in Chief (N00PA)
250 Makalapa Drive
Pearl Harbor, HI 96860-3131
(808) 471-3769
Web site: http://www.cpf.navy.mil

Due to the changing nature of Internet links, the Rosen Publishing Group, Inc., has developed an online list of Web sites related to the subject of this book. This site is updated regularly. Please use this link to access the list:

http://www.rosenlinks.com/wds/ugsd/

For Further Reading

Burgan, Michael. *Nuclear Submarines*. Mankato, MN: Capstone Press, 2001.

Burgan, Michael. *Submarines*. Mankato, MN: Capstone Press, 1998.

Genat, Robert, and Robin Genat. *Modern U.S. Navy Submarines*. Osceola, WI: Motorbooks International Publishers, 1997.

Lawliss, Chuck. *The Submarine Book: An Illustrated History of the Attack Submarine*. Short Hills, NJ: Burford Books, 2000.

Maas, Peter. *The Terrible Hours: The Man Behind the Greatest Submarine Rescue in History*. New York: HarperCollins Publishers, 2001.

Payan, Gregory. *Fast-Attack Submarine: The Seawolf Class*. New York: Children's Press, 2000.

Payan, Gregory, and Alexander Guelke. *Life on a Submarine*. New York: Children's Press, 2000.

Tall, J. J. *Submarines*. New York: Barron's Juveniles, 1998.

Bibliography

Barron's Educational Series, Inc. *The History of Submarines*. New York: Barron's Publishing, 1998.

Bricking, Tanya. "*Greeneville*'s Skipper Apologizes to Families of Victims." HonoluluAdvertiser.com. March 9, 2001. Retrieved August 2001 (http://the.honoluluadvertiser.com/2001/Mar/09/39localnews12.html).

Bricking, Tanya. "Rescued Crew's Plea: Find the Others." HonoluluAdvertiser.com. February 14, 2001. Retrieved August 2001 (http://the.honoluluadvertiser.com/2001/Feb/14/214localnews45.html).

Clancy, Tom. *Submarine: A Guided Tour Inside a Nuclear Warship*. New York: Berkley Publishing Group, 1993.

CNN.com "Japan Anger Grows over Sub Collision." February 14, 2001. Retrieved August 2001 (http://www.cnn.com/2001/WORLD/asiapcf/east/02/14/japan.sub.01).

CNN.com. "NTSB: Sub Crew Distracted by Civilians." February 21, 2001. Retrieved August 2001 (http://www.cnn.com/2001/US/02/21/japan.sub/index.html).

CNN.com. "Sources: Sub's Sonar Detected Other Vessel." February 20, 2001. Retrieved August 2001 (http://www.cnn.com/2001/US/02/20/japan.sub.03/index.html).

The USS *Greeneville* Submarine Disaster

Craven, John Pina. *The Silent War: The Cold War Battle Beneath the Sea*. New York: Simon and Schuster, 2001.

Friedman, Norman. *U.S. Submarines Since 1945: An Illustrated Design History*. Annapolis, MD: U.S. Naval Institute, 1994.

Online NewsHour. "Civilians On Board." March 5, 2001. Retrieved September 2001 (http://www.pbs.org/newshour/bb/military/jan-june01/sub_3-5.html).

Rosenfeld, Kayla. *Ehime Maru*. National Public Radio. Retrieved November 8, 2001 (http://www.npr.org).

Sontag, Sherry, Christopher Drew, and Annette Lawrence Drew. *Blind Man's Bluff: The Untold Story of American Submarine Espionage*. New York: HarperCollins Publishers, 2000.

U.S. Pacific Fleet Public Affairs. "Divers Locate, Recover Eighth Set of Remains." U.S. Navy's *Ehime Maru* Recovery Page. October 25, 2001. Retrieved November 2001 (http://www.cpf.navy.mil/CPFNEWS/0110recovery20.html).

U.S. Pacific Fleet Public Affairs. "Salvage Decision to Be Based on Technical Feasibility." U.S. Navy's *Ehime Maru* Recovery Page. February 19, 2001. Retrieved November 2001 (http://www.cpf.navy.mil/cpfnews/0102greeneville23.html).

Waller, Douglas C. *Big Red: Three Months Onboard a Trident Nuclear Submarine*. New York: HarperCollins Publishers, 2001.

Wright, Walter. "Coast Guard Promises to Keep Searching Until Hope Runs Out." HonoluluAdvertiser.com. February 11, 2001. Retrieved November 2001 (http://www.thehonoluluadvertiser.com/2001/Feb/11/211breaking6.html).

Index

B
Brandhuber, Captain Robert, 19, 33
Bush, President George W., 6–7
Bushnell, David, 9

C
Coen, Lieutenant Michael, 16, 18–19
Coffman, Douglas, 33
Commander Submarine Force, Pacific Fleet, 27

D
Drebbel, Cornelius van, 9

E
Ehime Maru, 5–7, 18–19, 21–23, 24
   captain of, 12
   collision/sinking of, 21–23, 29, 30, 31
   passengers on, 6, 25, 26, 39–40
   recovery efforts, 34–35, 36–40
   rescue mission, 25, 26–27
   as training vessel, 6, 9

I
Inoue, Masami, 33

J
Japan–United States relations, 6–7, 39

K
Konetzni, Albert, 31

M
McGiboney, Edward, 33
Mizuguchi, Takeshi, 39–40

O
Onishi, Hisao, 12

P
Pearl Harbor, Hawaii, 5, 16
Pfeifer, Lieutenant Commander Gerald, 33

S
Scorpio II, 34, 36
Seacrest, Petty Officer Patrick, 18, 19
sonar, how it works, 17
submarines, 9–13
   chain of command on, 12–13
   early history of, 9–10
   how they work, 11
   sonar and, 17, 20

The USS Greeneville Submarine Disaster

T
Tanabe, George, 37, 38

U
United States Coast Guard, 25
United States Navy Distinguished Visitors Program, 8, 33
USS *Greeneville*, collision with *Ehime Maru*
 civilian passengers and, 8, 15, 16, 19, 21, 23, 31, 33
 deaths resulting from, 5, 25
 navy inquiry into, 28–29, 30–33
 rescue mission, 25, 26–27
 sequence of events, 15–17, 18–23
 survivor/eyewitness accounts of, 7, 12, 23, 29
Uwajima Fisheries High School, 6

W
Waddle, Commander Scott, 7, 16, 18–23, 25, 26–27, 39
 apologizing for accident, 27–28
 military career of, 14
 and navy inquiry into accident, 28–29, 31–33
 punishment received, 32
Waddle, Jill, 27

About the Author
Eric Fein writes and edits books for children and young adults.

Photo Credits
Cover, pp. 1, 4–5, 6, 11, 18, 26, 28, 29, 34, 37, 38 © AP/Wide World Photos; p. 9 © Bettmann/Corbis; pp. 13, 20, 21, 40 © AFP/Corbis; p. 17 © Yogi, Inc./Corbis; p. 32 © US Navy.

Series Design and Layout
Les Kanturek

www.ingramcontent.com/pod-product-compliance
Lightning Source LLC
Chambersburg PA
CBHW041117070526
44584CB00002B/196